SKIP, SKIP, HOORAY!

Published by Crane Books

A Division of Crane Books Publishing, LLC

Murrieta, California

Printed in the United States of America

First Edition — 2025

ISBN 978-1-969705-16-8 (pbk)

www.CraneBooks.com

CRANE
BOOKS

It was a beautiful Saturday morning, and Julia had just finished her bowl of cereal. As she put her bowl in the dishwasher, she walked past the refrigerator, noticing the family pictures on the door.

She was missing her older brother Scott. He had joined the Army over a year ago and was stationed in Germany. The picture reminded her of the fun walks and bike rides she used to take with him around the block. It gave her an idea.

She walked up to her mom, hugged her, and asked, "Would it be ok if I went on a bike ride around the block by myself?"

Mom looked surprised and said, "By yourself? Are you sure?"

Julia nodded. "Yes. I'm 10 years old now and I can do it. I will be home before you know it."

Mom smiled. "Alright. But be careful."

As she buckled her helmet, and stepped outside, Julia felt both excited and a little nervous. "Let the adventure begin!" she said to herself.

As she pedaled down the block, Julia rode over a pile of crispy brown leaves that had fallen from the oak tree branches above.

Crunch! Crunch! The crackle and snap of the dry leaves were music to her ears.

As she passed the big white house on the corner, she saw the yellow daffodils dancing in the breeze by the front porch. Her best friend, Ginger, lived there.

Julia was excited to go visit her soon because her rabbit just had five bunnies, and they all needed names.

As she pedaled down the block, the blue jays and magpies were flying overhead and caught Julia's attention. Looking ahead to turn left at the corner, something else caught her eye.

A crooked For Sale sign stood in the yard of the old blue house on the corner.

Julia paused as she read the sign, trying to remember the family who once lived there.

Just then, Julia thought she heard something. She stopped and got off her bike. She was curious and a little frightened.

"What is it?" she thought. It sounded like a sniff, then a sniffle, and then a whimper.

Was someone.... crying?

The sound was coming from the bushes near the right side of the porch.

The house was empty, so knocking on the door to ask for help was not an option. She could be brave, just this once, all by herself.

Julia could smell the fresh-cut grass as she slowly moved toward the bushes. She could hear a woodpecker pecking away in the palm tree over her head.

She hesitated before crouching down, slowly pulling back the bush, and peeking in.

The bright sun shining down made it difficult to see anything. Julia felt her arm muscles tense up, and she could actually feel her heartbeat in her chest.

She couldn't remember ever feeling so nervous.

She thought to herself, "What's making that sound? Is it a wolf? A coyote? Will it jump out at me?" She saw the eyes first. Brown, sad, and scared. Then something jumped out of the bushes.

A dog!

Julia gasped and fell to the ground. It looked just like the dog that chased her last year and knocked her off her bike. She remembered that the dog bit her leg and pulled her down to the ground.

Some friends chased the dog away, but Julia's mom took her to the doctor to make sure her leg was ok and nothing was broken. The doctor stopped the bleeding and bandaged her wound.

Nothing was broken. That day, Julia decided she didn't like dogs anymore.

With the memory of last year fresh in her mind, Julia didn't know what to do about the dog in front of her today. She thought, "Was this the same dog?" She worried, "Would this dog try to bite me?" Time seemed to stand still. The dog had its head on its paws and was looking up at Julia.

She had to convince herself that this was not the same dog that knocked her off her bike a year ago. She noticed the dog had a collar and a worn out leash, but no name tag. After calming down and taking a few deep breaths, she smiled and whispered to the dog, "Are you lost?"

Julia had seen a show on TV where dog owners put their hand out slowly when approaching a stray dog to make them feel comfortable. They turned their body to the side and spoke softly.

She could do this, she told herself—no sudden moves. Julia crouched down low and slowly reached out to let the dog sniff her hand.

Her fear began to fade when the dog wagged its tail and looked as if it was smiling. She smiled in return, gently rubbed the dog's head, and took hold of the leash. This was not the same dog that pulled her off her bike last year.

Her first thought was to bring the dog home with her. Julia remembered her brother bringing home pets from friends who could no longer care for them, and her parents let them stay.

They had a dog named Pal and a rat named Whiskers at home. The only pet her dad ever said no to was a tarantula. "Take it back!" Dad said. Julia felt good about this dog.

"Okay," she said softly, "you can come home with me." Julia got on her bike, and the two continued their journey around the block.

She held the leash gently, and the dog's eyes sparkled as it pranced happily beside her.

It felt strange to have a dog with her. Julia's friends knew she didn't like dogs. What would they say?

She decided right then and there that she would give this dog a chance at happiness and hoped her friends would do the same.

As she approached her house, Julia thought about what her mom would say to her when she walked through the back door with a dog.

When Julia opened the back door, her mom was there to greet her. She had a surprised look on her face. "A dog?" she asked.

"You brought home a dog? But you don't like dogs."

"This dog is different," Julia said. "She's lost and needs a new family."

Julia reached down to pet the dog. "She is a happy dog, and she likes me.

Can we keep her?"

Her mom responded, "What if someone is missing her?"

"If she were your dog, wouldn't you want to get her back?."

"Well, yes," Julia answered. "But if we don't find her owner, can I keep her? I'll feed her and take her out for walks. I will take good care of her."

Her mom paused before answering, "We'll see."

The next day, Julia and her mom gave the dog a warm, soapy bath to get her clean before going to the vet. They hoped the vet could find a tiny microchip that might help them locate the dog's owner. Julia couldn't wait to find out if she could keep this happy dog or if she belonged to someone else.

Once inside the exam room, the vet looked at the dog and began the basic physical exam. She looked at her teeth, ears, skin, and eyes. She smiled when she finished and said, "Well, the good news is she is a healthy dog. No injuries. No fleas. No ticks."

Julia beamed!

Then the vet looked directly at Julia's mom and said, "I don't see a microchip. I don't know who she belongs to. If you decide to keep her, I strongly suggest you get her a microchip for identification and medical records." Her mom agreed, and they all walked out to the car.

Julia named the dog Scout, the perfect name for a brave dog. She spent the rest of the day playing with her, feeding her, and teaching her how to sit and lie down.

When it was time for bed, Scout curled up on a blanket next to Julia's bed. This made Julia smile as she pet her new friend behind the ears and said, "I think I'm really starting to like you."

Julia thought they would both sleep well, but that didn't go as planned. She had a dream about Scout's owner wanting her back.

This woke her up, and she looked right down at Scout. She called her name and tapped the bed, hoping Scout would jump up and join her. She hopped up on the bed and gave Julia a snuggle before they both fell asleep.

The next morning, Julia and Scout walked into the kitchen where her mom was working on the computer. "What are you doing?" Julia asked.

Found dog

"I am posting a picture of Scout on our neighborhood social media link to see if she belongs to anyone," her mom replied. "Her owners must be missing her, and we have to try to find them."

Julia knew her mom was right. She was hoping to find them...

But also hoping not to find them. Julia and Scout were becoming good friends, and she didn't want to give her up. Just then, Scout barked, and this reminded her that it was time to take her outside and get some food ready for her breakfast.

DOG FOOD

A few days later, Julia and Scout were sitting on the front porch steps, watching the cars drive by.

"I miss my brother, Scott," she said softly. The dog's left ear perked up. Julia blinked. "Scott," she said again. Now the right ear perked up.

"Wait... is your name Scott? Scottie?" The dog jumped up and put her paws on Julia's legs, tail wagging wildly.

"Your name *is* Scottie! Just like my brother." She hoped Scottie would meet Scott one day. She knew they would like each other right away. Scottie had a way with people.

Two joyful weeks passed. Julia and Scottie went on many adventures together. They went for walks, worked on a handshake to show everyone, and even met some new dog friends.

Scottie got along with just about everyone, except the dog across the street. That dog liked to bark at Scottie. Sometimes Scottie barked back, but most of the time, she kept walking by Julia's side.

One Saturday morning, a lady called Julia's mom regarding Scottie. Her name was Betsy, and she lived across town.

She had seen the post that was made online and knew instantly that Scottie was her dog. Betsy and Julia's mom set up a day and time to meet and return Scottie.

Julia's heart sank. She had grown to love Scottie. She loved feeding her, playing with her, and taking her for walks. Every day was a new adventure.

Scottie had truly become part of the family. Her tail wagged happily each morning, she snored softly at night, and she danced beside Julia, as if they always belonged together.

But Julia knew that someone else loved Scottie and was deeply missing her. Betsy's phone call to her mom had made that clear. Somewhere, across town, Betsy was excited to hear Scottie's happy bark, take her for walks, and feel her warm snuggles.

Julia knew what she had to do. With tears stinging in her eyes, she gathered Scottie's blanket and food bowl, her new leash, and the squeaky duck toy she played with every afternoon. She hugged Scottie tight, burying her face in Scottie's soft fur.

"Be brave, sweet girl," she whispered. "You're going home." Then Julia, Scottie, and her mom climbed into the car for the long drive across town. Julia held Scottie's paw and wished time would slow down just a little.

Julia and her mom pulled up to Betsy's Animal Shelter. There was a worn-out sign in front and the chain-link fence leaned to one side. Blue paint was peeling off the front door. The grass was patchy and dry, and a few dog toys lay near the front door.

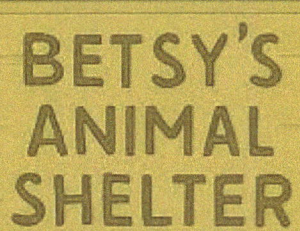

Scottie stood up and looked out the window. Did she recognize this place? Her tail gave one quick wave before it suddenly stopped.

Julia noticed one of the windows was covered with wood instead of glass.
From inside, they could hear dogs barking. "Were these dogs Scottie's friends?" she wondered.

This wasn't the warm, happy place Julia had imagined. She looked at her mom, and then back to Scottie, who was staring at the shelter with her eyes wide open. "It's OK, girl," Julia whispered, "I'm right here." Julia took a deep breath and gently clipped on Scottie's leash, hoping she was doing the right thing.

The front door opened, and Betsy stood on the doorstep with a happy look on her face. As soon as the car door opened, Scottie jumped out and pulled Julia with her to greet Betsy. They were so excited to see each other again. After a quick hello, Scottie moved back to sit by Julia, torn between the two people she loved.

They all walked inside the shelter together and sat down on the sofa. Julia noticed a photo of a soldier in a frame on the table.

"Who's that?" Julia asked.

"That's my son, Richard," Betsy said. "He is on a secret mission. They cannot tell me where he is, and I really miss him."

"My older brother, Scott, is in the Army," Julia added. "He is stationed in Germany, and he is a mechanic. I miss him, too. I named the dog Scottie, after my brother."

Julia hugged Scottie and looked at Betsy, who was watching them both.

Betsy smiled and said, "I can tell how much you love Scottie. If you'd like to give her a home, she's yours. She'll need plenty of attention, food, space to walk, and a toy to play with. Can you give her that?"

"Yes, I can do that!" She replied.

On the drive home, Julia asked her mom about the shelter. Her mom explained that the animals were cared for, but the building itself needed some repairs. It could use a fresh coat of paint, new grass, a new window, and better spaces for the animals to be safe and happy.

Julia thought for a moment. "Mom, what if we helped fix it up? Maybe we could save the shelter?"

Her mom reached over and squeezed her hand. "I love that idea! Maybe we could ask our friends, or even get your school involved. Imagine how happy those animals would be!"

By the time they reached home, the two of them started making a plan. Scottie wagged her tail as if she already knew - something wonderful was about to happen.

On Monday, Julia and her mom met with the principal after school to share their idea on how to help the shelter.

The annual school carnival was approaching, and Julia asked, "Can we have a booth for Betsy's Animal Shelter, where she could bring some of her animals for adoption? I can ask my classmates to help paint signs and hand out flyers." Mom added, "We can share information on the school web page about how to adopt pets and help clean up the shelter."

The principal loved the idea, "What a wonderful way to help our community," she said, smiling. "Let's make it happen!"

Word spread quickly through the school. Students volunteered to paint posters, make donation jars, and decorate the booth with paw prints and hearts. Julia's class offered to collect pet food, blankets, and dog toys.

The day of the carnival had finally arrived, and the school campus was filled with excitement. Near the center of it all stood the new booth for Betsy's Animal Shelter. Julia and her mom hung up a bright banner that read, "Paws for a Cause!"

While her friends set out water bowls and toys for the visiting animals, Betsy arrived with cheerful puppies, a sleepy cat, and a playful pug.

Families stopped to pet the animals and learn about the shelter. In the cafeteria, Sergeant Stevens volunteered to run the Bingo games.

He led the cheers when players won, shouting, "BINGO for Betsy!" This made everyone laugh. But instead of keeping their prize money, people donated their winnings to help Betsy's Animal Shelter.

Through the community's generosity, there was enough money to give the shelter a fresh coat of paint, repair the window, clean up the cages, and plant new grass. Julia could hardly believe it - what started as a small idea was now a big act of kindness that would truly make a difference.

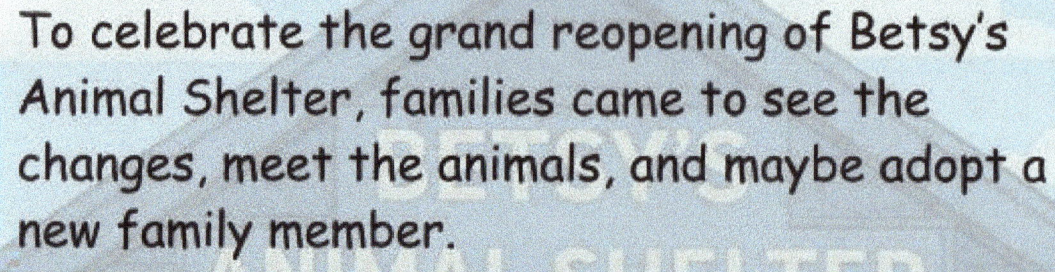

To celebrate the grand reopening of Betsy's Animal Shelter, families came to see the changes, meet the animals, and maybe adopt a new family member.

The shelter looked brand new with bright blue paint, a new window, beautiful flowers along the walkway, and fresh green grass.

Sergeant Stevens was there, proudly wearing his uniform, and helping Betsy, Julia, and Scottie greet visitors by the front gate.

Laughter and cheerful barks filled the air as families played with the dogs in the yard.

Then Sergeant Stevens stepped forward to make a special announcement.

"There are two special recruits who flew a long way to be here today," he said. Everyone turned toward the parking lot as a car door opened and two familiar faces appeared.

Julia gasped - she could hardly believe her eyes.

It was her brother Scott and Betsy's son Richard! Julia's eyes filled with happy tears as she raced up to Scott with Scottie running beside her.

She threw her arms around him and hugged him tight, feeling her brother's love she had missed for so long. Scottie barked and wagged her tail like she remembered him, too.

Betsy hurried over and wrapped her arms around Richard, both of them laughing and crying at the same time.

The crowd clapped and cheered as the two families reunited. Sergeant Stevens smiled proudly, watching the joyful scene unfold. Julia smiled, knowing this was a day she'd always remember. It was about love, family, and the magic of kindness that brought a community together.

As the sun began to set, Julia looked around at the happy families, wagging tails, and smiling faces. Scottie rested her head on Julia's lap, and her heart felt full as she watched her brother talk to his friends.

This all started with one small act of kindness and a dog named Scottie.

Her mom came over and sat down next to Julia. She put a loving arm around her and said, "See what happens when you Show Kindness In Person?"

Julia smiled. "Yep," she said. "It makes the world a better place – one SKIP at a time."

SKIP Discussion Questions:

1. How many acts of kindness did you see in the book?

2. Why do you think Julia and her mom decided to help the animal shelter?

3. What does the animal shelter's transformation teach us about teamwork and caring for animals?

4. What can you do to help an animal shelter in your community?

5. What does it mean to Show Kindness In Person? (SKIP)

Julia and Scottie encourage children to Show Kindness In Person through teamwork, compassion, and empathy. Perfect for classrooms, families, and grouip discussions, this story inspires students to S.K.I.P. with classmates, friends, and loved ones. When we work together, kindness can spread beyond the page.

The S.K.I.P. Mission:

Show Kindness In Person - one kind act at a time.

How will you S.K.I.P. today?

Dedication:

This book is dedicated to my mom, Margaret Bullock, a former special education teacher. She taught me to love books, embrace life and family, seek out every adventure, and work hard without ever giving up. Her strength, joy, and unwavering love continue to inspire me every day.

www.ingramcontent.com/pod-product-compliance
Lightning Source LLC
Chambersburg PA
CBHW051851140626
46547CB00034BA/3210